AUTHENTIC

Unconventional Poetry
By A Woman Who Finally Embraces
Her Unconventional Self

By
Cindy Best

DEDICATION

To my two amazing sons, Ryan and Drew, who have always been my sunshine and who have taught me unconditional love.
I love you both to the mountains and back.

To my Mom and Dad who have given me my roots and wings, and have always been the wind beneath my wings.

Love you all.

So blessed to have you all in my life.

POETRY

I wrote my first poem today
and it set me free
the words rumbling inside me
for so long
burst out of my chest
and onto these pages
so I begin
yet another chapter.

ROOTS AND WINGS

Being a Mom is like giving birth to a huge piece of your heart
and then giving it to the world.
Raising a child with special needs
is giving to the very depth of your heart and soul.
You find your strength as a Mom
to be the rock around which your child plants their roots.
You become the Mother Bear
protecting your cub against the bullies and injustices of the world.
You fight to have their special gifts realized in themselves.
You teach them independence
and how to advocate for themselves.
And then you do the hardest thing of all...
you let go...
having given them roots...
watching them grow their wings.

DIVORCE

You left because you wanted a true home
a peaceful place to raise your children.
You wanted to feel like yourself again
no longer wanting to listen to the doubts he
planted in your head
and your heart
because you were tired of riding the roller
coaster
the ups and downs of this toxic relationship.
You gave everything you had
and it still wasn't enough.
You are beyond exhausted...
mentally, physically, emotionally.
You deserve to be appreciated for the
loving wife, amazing mom
and all around family rock that you are.
You shouldn't have to do it all
marriage is a partnership...
remember?
You knew it would be harder to do it alone.
You are so scared to hurt your children

but you are even more afraid of losing
yourself
completely disappearing
and then you realize
it is better for your children
to wrestle with the hurt of divorce
than lose their mom completely
because she could no longer
hear her own voice,
feel her own worth
and be herself

BE BRAVE

Be brave enough
to be yourself
to hear your own voice
forge your own path
be kind to yourself
to give your heart to the world
to create your own life
on your own terms
with work that sums up
your purpose and your passion
while allowing you to stay balanced.
Be brave enough
to be a true blue
marble jar friend
who gives and receives equally.
Be brave enough
to be a true partner
who sets and respects boundaries
who can remain yourself
by saying NO kindly
and remembering to save pieces of your
heart and soul

for yourself.
Be who you are.
Embrace all of your pieces.
Be in this life on purpose.
Be brave.

CONVENTION

Convention is like a wool sweater that has
shrunk in the dryer.
It's tight
and itchy.
You're dying to take it off.
I pull at the 1 rogue yarn
and unravel it
completely
til in unfurls on the ground
1 long, winding string.
I rub it til it's soft and felted.
I take up my needles and begin anew
knitting a sweater that feels right
that's a good fit for me.
It is a tight knit sweater
full of strength
from interweaving the connections of family
and the empowering fibers of a great circle
of friends.
It has purpose
is made with passion and hard work
just like my life.

I did drop a stitch
there is a hole where the love of my life
should be.
I tug at the yarn
unraveling the missed stitch
filling in that hole with self love and
appreciation.
When I am done
it is a sweater of warmth and comfort.
It's only itch is for adventure
and the only piece missing
is the 1 round button of a man
made of weathered wood
strong enough to connect all of the pieces
of me
holding me together at the top
yet confident enough
to let me blow in the breeze at the bottom
as my independent self

FRIENDSHIP GARDEN

As I've gotten older
my friendship garden
has gotten smaller
on purpose.
I've realized
that in order to grow
you need to occasionally weed
your friendship garden
pulling the superficial friends
pruning off the energy suckers
making the shitty friends into compost
putting your energy
into your true blue friends
friends who give and receive equally
your friends who play in the mud with you
drink in the water and nutrients alongside
you
so together you can grow in the sunshine.

FAVORITE JEANS

I want a man
who is like my favorite pair of jeans
weathered from the sun
made of tough denim
but soft from wear
torn at the knees from hard work
trim at the waist from self care
strong, yet flexible
a few earthly treasures in his pockets
a man confident enough
to put on his own boxer briefs
but vulnerable enough to let me take them off
ready to love me with everything he's got
strong enough to let me
put on my own "big girl" panties
but gentle enough to take them off
appreciating me baring my heart and soul
and ready to love him with all I've got
and when our connection is complete
willing to step into those favorite jeans
equally

each of us
strong individuals
connected by common threads
and true partnership.

SEPARATE CABINS

Oh love
don't take it personally
that I believe
the secret
to a good relationship
is separate cabins.
It has nothing to do with you
and everything to do with me.
I have learned
that I am a woman
who needs her space
and her own place.
I create my space on purpose
every object and piece of furniture
strategically placed
to create an environment
of light and peace.
Chaos and drama are not welcome here.
So if that is what you've got
in your overnight bag
you can just go
and don't look back.

No one fucks with my peace
ever again.
Don't get me wrong
I am happy to share my space
when I am recharged and ready.
I am capable of sharing space.
I did it for 15 years in a marriage.
I did it for 25 years as a parent.
I did it for 2 years with my last love.
But just because I invite you into my cabin
doesn't mean you can unpack and stay
forever.
I am a girl who needs her own space
beyond Virginia Wolf's belief
that every woman needs a room of her own.
Get out from under my roof.
Beyond Katherine Hepburn's theory
of "live next door, but visit often".
Get out of my yard.
My little log cabin in the woods
is my sanity.
The garden's surrounding it...
my paradise.

The pottery studio and the blacksmith forge...
my fire and creativity.
I am so happy to share all of that with you
open my heart to you
share my beautiful soul with you
and if the deep connection is there
even share my bed with you.
But in order to do that
you must be comfortable with yourself
confident enough to know
I am not going anywhere.
I am a woman who gives away
a lot of energy to my family, my friends,
my love and the amazing students I work with.
The only way for that to be sustainable
is to take time to recharge
regroup
alone.
So, my love, don't take it personally.
It has nothing to do with you
and everything to do with me.

I just need you to be strong enough to realize
the secret to a good relationship with me is separate cabins.

I DON'T PLAY GAMES

I am a girl
who doesn't play games.
Didn't do high school politics as a teenager
refuse to do them as a grown woman.
I wear my heart on my sleeve.
I don't have a poker face.
I have lost all of my marbles
and lay all of my cards on the table.
I don't do on line dating
and I can spot a player a mile away.
I have learned to play with a full deck
holding my hearts close,
clubbing my demons,
calling a spade a spade,
and finding diamonds in the rough.
I am a girl who doesn't play games.

LOTUS FLOWER

I am the lotus flower
rooted in the mess and mud of life
growing in spite of all that shit
into a flower of distinction
unique color
individual beauty
and wisdom
always stretching
toward the light.

Namaste.

THE MEN I'VE LOVED

One needed a mom to run his life
and to finally grow up.
One needed sobriety.
One needed freedom.
One needed a girl to wear the pants.
One needed children of his own.
One needed Viagra.
Now I've done it.
NO MAN will ever be brave enough
to love me
knowing I will always tell the truth.

THE UNCONVENTIONAL POET

Writing a good poem
is as satisfying as great sex.
There is a whole lot of connection
followed by sweet release.

EMPTY NEST

My oldest child turned 25 today.
I can't even call him a child anymore.
He is a man.
an amazing man.
My other son is 20
also no longer a child
and growing into another amazing man.
I am so grateful for my two sons.
They are beautiful inside and out.
It seems impossible
that I have been a parent for 25 years
almost half my life.
It feels like yesterday
that they were little bundles in my arms
and just setting out to explore this world.
Now their explorations take them further
away from home...
college, real jobs, travel, adventure.
The nest I so carefully built for them
is now empty.
Our little log cabin where I raised them
along with our 3 cats and a dog

always felt so crowded with all of us in it.
Now it's just me and 2 cats.
I clean it and it stays clean for days
weeks even.
I no longer have dinners to cook every night
lunches to pack
keep track of where everyone needs to be
and when.
And as much as that exhausted me
I miss it.
I miss them
their energy
their mischief
their hugs
their smiles.
My boys
who have grown into amazing, kind, creative,
hard working, loving men.
My boys
who tower over me
making me the short one in the family.
I gave them their roots
now I watch them from the nest
as they take flight

finding their wings
in this great big world.
My nest feels empty.
Now it is time for me to take flight
enjoy some freedom
and rediscover
my own wings.

REAR VIEW MIRROR

What are you going to do,
leave me and be a fuckin' potter?
Those are the words you said to me
as I drove away with our 2 boys
watching you in the rear view mirror.
Stuck
unwillinging to grow
to change
to accept responsibility
to take a good long look at yourself.
For I was stuck too
but I sought out help
to learn to see myself again
to sort out the pieces of myself
to accept responsibility
for my part in our broken relationship.
I have grown.
I have changed.
I have found myself again...
the girl that got so lost in marriage,
motherhood, work...
doing it all

being it all
for everybody
all of the time.
I don't want to be lost anymore.
I have worked too hard
to be found again.
I have realized that I need to be
my strong self
to be the best mother.
I need to be my authentic self
to be balanced
working in a job I love and create
that allows me to keep my sanity
while raising 2 boys
on my own
in peace.
You call me crazy
for being on meds and in therapy.
But the truth is
I am the sane one.
I choose sanity.
I choose growth.
I choose change.
I choose balance.

I choose peace.
I choose my children.
I choose poverty
in order to be rich in other ways.
I choose to leave behind
your chaos and drama
and watch you fade away
in my rear view mirror.

BOUNDARIES

Setting and sticking to boundaries
is how we keep ourselves
and our relationships healthy.
Why then
am I always the bitch
for setting clear boundaries
and sticking to them?
If you don't get boundaries,
then I don't want you in my life.
I would rather be
The Boundary Bitch
than go back to being
The Door Mat.

SOUL SISTER

We drive cross country
in my van
without a plan
allowing the Moms in us
the freedom to just let go
let it unfold
wake up and decide where we want to go
today.
For 25 years
we have raised children.
Always with a plan
every move thought out.
But today and for the next few weeks
we are free.
We are just you and me.
Soul Sisters
The only friend I could live in a van
and a tent with for weeks.
Finding adventure around every turn.
Living out of our cooler
little money but lots of time
and open road.

We let it unfold.
Crying together as we leave behind
the hardships of the last year.
Marveling in our children
and how hard it is to let them go.
Rediscovering ourselves.
2 creative, adventurous girls
who are not afraid to live their dreams
who are embracing this new found freedom
together.
We sing out loud
and off key
just you and me
as we drive West.
We laugh.
We brainstorm.
We dream.
We live out loud,
on purpose,
by the seat of our pants
and on the change in our pockets.
Discovering new places
rediscovering ourselves
deepening our friendship.

I love you
my Soul Sister.

UNCONVENTIONAL POEMS
-continued-

The words keep coming
pouring out in waves
forming these unconventional poems
that may not be what the literary world
would call them
maybe ramblings of an ADHD brain
call them what you want
for me, they are powerful
they have purpose
and I am grateful
that the words keep coming.

GIRLFRIENDS ARE THE GLUE

In my experience
other than my Dad
and my sons
men come and go
but it is my true blue girlfriends
my Mom and sister included
that are the glue
that hold me together
when everything feels
like it is falling apart.

ALL MY MARBLES ROLL SOUTH TO THE CAPE

Throughout the years
there have been many times
that I've felt like
I've lost it
I've finally lost all of my marbles
but that's okay
because now I know
they all roll south to The Cape.
I start finding them again
as soon as I pack up
and pull out of the driveway
as soon as I roll my windows down
to breathe in the salt air
as soon as I drive over the Sagamore Bridge
singing the Indigo Girls Closer I Am To Fine.
But for me
The Cape doesn't start
til you pass the Orlean's rotary
the windmill in Eastham
Coast Guard Beach where you can walk forever

the village of Wellfleet
hiking out to Great Isle at low tide
trekking through the dunes of Truro
wandering the streets of P-town
watching the seals play at Race Point
going in mid-September
when the tourists are gone
living like a local
warm enough for a bathing suit during the day
cool enough for a sweater at night
as you watch the sun sink into the ocean.
All of my marbles are there.
I find them among the heart shaped rocks
and the sea glass.
I feel them in the sunshine on my face
and the wind in my hair.
I rediscover them when I wiggle my toes in the sand
do yoga on the beach
walk miles in the sun
paddle board in the bay
and swim in the surf.
I collect my marbles

one by one
and when my jar is full
and it's time to go home
I roll my windows down
breathe in the salt air
feel the wind in my hair
one more time
crossing the bridge
singing and feeling Closer I Am To Fine.
I know where my marbles are.
They are not lost
they've just rolled South to The Cape.

FAMILY TREE

It is my Mom
who always said
as a parent
your job is to give your children
roots and wings.
Ah Mom
you are a wise woman
for you and Dad
taught me through your amazing parenting
how to find my own roots
in our family tree
how to grow my branches
as I headed out into the world
how to feel my wings
when it was time to be brave
grow
change
fly in a new direction
and when I built my own nest
in the branches of our family tree
those words and your example
taught me how to give

my own children
roots and wings.

LEARNING TO FLY

Aerial yoga
Crap
I think I signed up for the wrong class!
I envisioned
restorative poses in a swing of silk
not cirque du soleil moves
hanging upside down
trusting the seat of my yoga pants
legs wrapped around suspended silks!
Why am I so afraid?
Because I have to let go
but slowly
through practice
I realize
I am not too old for this.
I am stronger than I thought
braver than I knew
adventurous enough to fly.
I have learned to let go.

BOOK WORM

Looking for me?
I am the girl still in bed
lingering over a cup of coffee
my nose in a good book.
I set my alarm a little early
just so I can sneak in a chapter
before I start my day.
I head to bed a little earlier
just to get in
one more chapter before I fall asleep.
There is a towering stack of books
on my night stand
another on the floor.
I love the site of the written word.
I love the feel of the page as I turn it.
Forget Kindle.
It's just not the same for me.
There is nothing like a good
Nothing Til Noon Sunday
reading in bed
coffee in a mug
a good book

my journal
and The Sunday Times in hand.
There is nothing like the smell of the library
wandering the isles of your favorite book store...
sorry trees!
for I need my words on paper
tangible
so grateful for your sacrifice
so I can be
a book worm.

CREATE

There is nothing like the feeling
of creating something from nothing
but the visions in your head
the fire in your soul
and your own 2 hands.
When I create
is when I feel most
ALIVE.

BE

Be the change
you want to see in the world
for you were made
on purpose
every part
every piece
every wire
every connection
created on purpose
as you.
Take those special gifts
your parts and pieces
your unique wiring
roll them up into a ball
wind up
and throw yourself out into the world.
Start small
be the pebble
tossed into the pond
creating ripples
encouraged by the wind
led by the watershed

to the ocean
to turn into waves
waves of change
that make a difference
out in this world.
Be
all that you are made of.
Be you.

CHANGE

Life is change
growth is optional
so true
choose
change
grow
for without change
we are stuck
stagnant
dying.
When we embrace change
we learn
we grow
we live.
Be brave enough to change.

WHERE ARE ALL THE REAL WOMEN?

Where are all the real women?
I haven't seen them around town
in their tailored clothes,
manicured hands and fancy cars
for these are not the real women.
The real women
are found next to you
in the trenches
wrestling their way
through the mud
through the messiness of life,
love, work and family.
They have mud on their faces
dirt under their fingernails
and clay in their hair.
They are tired but satisfied
after a long day of work.
They are cranky.
They are up then down
left then right
riding the rollercoaster of life
with their hands in the air...

screaming
smiling in their hearts
and building fires in their souls.
These are the real women.
These are the women I choose to surround
myself with.

MUSIC

Music
feeds my soul
fuels my heart
helps me to let go
dig deep
feel
music is my favorite therapy
just need to turn the dial
pop in a cd
or drop the needle
on your favorite vinyl
and slowly
you become yourself again

FEED YOUR SOUL

Feed your soul
not your head
with drugs and misconceptions
numbing the pain
the feelings
for the only way to truly be
is to feel your way through the pain
make yourself feel
feed your head with knowledge then
Learn
Feel
Grow
Dig deep
Find your fire
Feel your wings
Feed your soul

COURAGE

Courage
Find it
Feel it
Use it
Don't lose it

JUST BE YOU

Be peaceful
Be graceful
Be wild
Untamed
and free
Just Be You

GETTING OLDER

I like getting older
it is when you become
comfortable in your own skin
appreciate who you are
you find out what really makes you tick
you stop giving a shit
about what other people think
you learn what to let go of
and who to hold onto
you live life on your own terms
and are finally true to yourself

PRACTICE

Practice patience
and you will get there
in your own time
in your own way
remembering how hard you've worked
how far you've come

UNTAMED

Find the few people
that have the courage
to love
what is untamed
in you

MESSAGE FROM THE UNIVERSE

Don't try to figure out the HOWs of it
that is not your job
you only need to know
WHAT you want
then just follow your instincts
and let the universe
figure out the HOWs
Think
Think
and Let Go

DREAMS

Dreams are like eggs
we need to be patient
keep them warm
and alive
until they are ready
to hatch

THE BOX

We're not supposed to fit
inside the box
there's no room for growth
in there
no matter how hard
you try to squeeze me in
I am not going to fit
I am the turbulent indigo crayon
that will bend and break
if I try to fit inside the box.
I prefer the freedom of the great big world
outside of the box!

SUNFLOWERS

With the earth below
and the blue sky above
sunflowers radiate
pure unconditional love
close your eyes
visualize the life you want to live
plant the seeds
embrace every moment
as a chance to love,
give and grow

HOPE FLOATS

You may feel
like you are sinking
but remember
hope floats

ALONE

One week
alone at The Cape
in a little cabin
in the woods
finding my footing
reawakening myself
collecting my marbles
the best gift I have ever given myself
I yearn for it
all year long

50

50 is when
you finally know who you are
believe in yourself
know what you want
finally say what you mean
and mean what you say
and for the first time in your life
choose you

BROKEN

We are all broken
in different places
use those cracks to let the light in
don't be afraid of the darkness
in yourself
use it to help you find your light
and once you find it
feed it with the fire in your heart
the warmth in your soul
blow on it 'til you've set the world on fire
burn bright
shine
set yourself free from your fear.

MEN

I have raised
1 husband
2 sons
and 3 boyfriends...
I am exhausted!
Are there any men out there
who are actually
passionate
creative
enjoy nature
appreciate a simple little life
crave a little adventure
have a soul and a spiritual side
are positive
have their finances together
are independent
like time alone
love children but don't want any more of
their own
are honest

hardworking
kind
faithful
strong
and believe in themselves
and in me?
If not, then I am happy to be alone.

HALF YOUR HEART

Sending your child
out into the world
is like cutting out
half of your heart
and then
letting it go.

SOUL MATE

Some day
I hope to find my soul mate.
Someone who likes me for me
loves me for all that I am
appreciates me
and doesn't take me for granted.
Someone to share a deep connection with
mentally, emotionally, physically and
spiritually
a true partner, lover and treasured member
of my family.
That is worth waiting for.
I will no longer accept less.
I will not lose myself again
for I like who I am
who I've become
the woman I've grown to be.
So until my soul mate crosses my path
I will continue moving forward
and enjoy just being me.

ADVICE FROM THE TRENCHES

Be honest and upfront in your relationships
If you have something hard to say
Be brave enough to say it anyway
Deliver it with kindness
in person
face to face
Fully appreciate the one you love
Don't ever take that love for granted
Give as much love and support as you are given
Be financially responsible
You have always had the ability to build your dreams
Now dig deep to find the discipline
Be resourceful
Be creative
Stop procrastinating
Be balanced with work and home life
Life is too short and too precious
to always be working
Set boundaries around your time
and what you are willing to give

Save a little something for yourself
in the name of self preservation
Be mindful of your drinking
and learn to be kinder to your body
Be open to not just providing therapy
but receiving it
Expand your mind and your heart
As a parent, don't shame, blame or judge
your child
Each child finds their way
in their own way and their own time
We are all created exactly how we are
on purpose
for a purpose
Be accepting of your child's differences
Give them roots and wings
Most of all
Dare to bring your dreams to life
Go be brave enough to build
the life you've always dreamed of.

IT'S REALLY SO SIMPLE

As my parents grow older
I realize what they need from me most
is presence not presents
a phone call
a visit
a simple I LOVE YOU.
When life is busy
and I feel too overwhelmed to call them
I remind myself
life is short
pick up the phone
call them anyway.
That small gift of time
is enough to make their day
and remind them that
they are loved and appreciated.
It's really so simple.

GUESS I WON'T BE RETIRING AS A WRITER

I did it!
I actually published my first book
with a real publisher
a signed contract
a dream fulfilled
I was brave enough
to put a piece of my heart and soul
out into the world
the payoff for this vulnerability is worth it
a quarterly commission check
a book signing
MY book on AMAZON and the publisher's website
positive reviews
and then I get that quarterly commission check
for 82 cents
At first I think
what was I thinking selling a piece of my soul for a 5% commission?
I guess I won't be retiring as a writer!

But then I realize
I didn't put this book out into the world to make money
That check for 82 cents is humbling
It is a reminder that the reason I wrote
MEET ME WHERE I'M AT
was to help just 1 child with special needs
to learn to advocate for themselves
and at 82 cents
I did just that
I gave 1 child a tool for their toolbox.
Mission accomplished!

TREASURE

The words
they churn inside me
like the sea
for days
weeks
sometimes months
until one day
they get caught up in the tide
ride the wave to shore
and land on the beach
in a treasure chest
full of gems
each one
a piece of my heart

DATE AT YOUR OWN RISK

You date a singer,
you may end up in a song.
You date a writer,
you may end up in a book.
You break an artist's heart
and the odds of ending up in their work
increases exponentially.
Guess maybe I should come with a warning label
"date at your own risk".

MOVING ON

Can past loves remain friends?
I guess not.
I always thought it was possible.
You give someone a piece of your heart
when you love them.
So even once it's over,
I always believed
that person still held a piece of your heart
and you held a piece of them in yours.
I thought I finally got it right
and that even though it was over
we could indeed
still be friends.
Not in an every day
in your life sense
or a still get together
and go places way
but in a comfortable, respectful,
considerate run into you
truly happy to see you and catch up
kind of way.
But now?

Now I'm just somebody that you used to know.
Maybe it's not possible after all.

GETTING OLD IS NOT FOR SISSIES

Getting old is not for sissies
that is why my girlfriends and I
have created our own "retirement plan".
We will live in little cottages at The Cape
close enough to trek our orthopedic shoes
& rolling walkers next door to check on each other.
We will raid each other's closets
when our spines shrink & our waists expand.
We will wear our glasses on beautiful
beaded strings around our neck so we no longer lose them.
We will enjoy our meals on wheels together
and beg our home health aides to paint our toenails
when we can no longer stretch that far.
We will drive our motorized scooters to the beach
and use our "I've fallen and I can't get up" buttons
around our neck when we get stuck in the sand.

We will pick each other up emotionally
and call the fire department to pick us up physically.
Together we will boycott going to a nursing home
and be there for each other with help from the Visiting Nurses and Hospice.
When our memories start to fade and our bodies betray us
we will accompany each other to Oregon
choosing to say goodbye in our own way
in our own time
having truly LIVED in our old age
leaving this world in the arms of our families
and holding the hands of our girlfriends.
We will go bravely, boldly into our next life.
No sissies here.

HURT

Hurt
It's usually the first thing I feel
when someone's actions affect me.
But later, after I've gone from hurt
to sadness
to pissed off
I realize that no,
that person did not walk in my shoes
before they acted to consider my feelings.
But that was because they were caught up
in their own feelings
and their actions actually had nothing to do
with me.
There was no intent to hurt my feelings,
no ill will.
They were caught in a moment and simply
reacted.
End of story.
Why then do our heads and our hearts
go right to hurt?

GIVING

I love to give.
It is a piece of who I am.
It brings me joy
gives me a sense of purpose.
But over the years
I realize I give too much.
When I give too much, I get exhausted.
When I give to someone, but they keep wanting more
I feel resentful and taken advantage of.
I realize now
that is my struggle with boundaries
...again...
damn this is a hard lesson!
So now I practice giving, but not giving too much.
Setting that boundary
that says "this is what I can give".
No longer offering an inch
and end up giving a yard.
When asked to give more
now I remember to say

"this is what I have to give".

ALL IS NOT LOST

Today
I met a strong, kind
and spirited man
who knows himself.
Who knows what will happen?
In all honesty,
it doesn't matter.
It's just reassuring to know
they are out there.
All is not lost!

LOG CABIN LIFE

I awake to crunching
outside my bedroom window.
Who is coming out of the woods
into my yard but a young female moose.
She stops and listens
as I gently talk to her.
My day off is spent
puttering in my garden
paddle boarding on the lake
and mountain biking through the woods.
The day ends with a mama bear
and her two cubs crossing my dirt road.
I live in paradise!
I love my peaceful little life.

FIRE

I create with clay
and forge with steel.
My work comes to life at 2000 degrees.
I am ignited by the sun
and drawn to the glow of the moon.
Fireflies wink at me
campfire ashes dance with me.
I am a girl
who likes to play with fire.

WATER

My toes push off
from the sandy bottom
as I launch into the water.
I ground my feet on the board
standing tall
feeling graceful.
The sway of the paddle board
calms me.
My body and breath
fall into rhythm.
I am called to the lake by the loons
embraced by the breeze
and kissed by the sun.
Balance restored.

MASSAGE

My body and spirit
are depleted
from so much giving.
The knots in my muscles
a testament
to giving it all away
forgetting again
to save a little something
for myself.
Your strong hands knead my muscles
releasing all that I have been holding on to
in every fiber of my being.
My right side feels so heavy
from all this giving.
As you move to the left side of my body
I resist all of this receiving.
It is practice for me to receive.
I give into it
realizing I am thirsty for it
and finally drink in
your healing energy.
As I leave your presence

I walk away taller,
grounded and calm.
Body realigned
Peace restored.
The tears begin to flow the next day
releasing all that I had stowed away
in my cells.
You've unlocked all of those
deep seeded emotions.
Thank you for your gift of touch
and being willing to share it.

THE WORDS

The words came to me
in the middle of the night
along with the breeze through my window
stirring me from my sleep
daring me to turn on the light
and write
I set my journal and pencil down
only to click the light back on
as the words keep coming
pouring out of me
as poems

THEY'RE BACK

They're back.
I turn on the light
AGAIN!
Having to capture these words
before I lose them.

PEACEFUL LITTLE LIFE

The cabin is my own again.
Quiet
Still
My youngest home from college
for the summer
but gone for the weekend.
His presence fills our cabin
with the ups and downs of being 20.
I embrace this feeling of peace
being back on my own time
not tethered to anyone.
It restores me.
The cool night breeze
reminds me
Fall is coming.
He will go back to school soon.
I must treasure this time
that he is home.
For I have learned
with my oldest son
there will come a time
when he'll have a life of his own

and rarely come home.
I am learning to appreciate all of this.
So I look forward
to the cabin being mine again.
My time completely my own.
The thought both terrifies and intrigues me.
For both of us
the possibilities are endless.
Adventure awaits.

THAT'S IT!

That's it!
I am turning out the light now!
WORDS
I am tired from you
tumbling out of me.
I am ready to FINALLY get some sleep.
Where the hell is the OFF switch?
Good night already!

CONNECTION

WOW
I had forgotten
what if felt like
to really connect with someone
that feeling of being wide awake
that hum throughout your body
all senses on high alert
your soulful eyes
your kind smile
broad muscles
and man bun
you had me at hello
the way you see the world
give to the world
are a kid magnet
and a wise old soul
I knew you were younger
Late 30's?
I could've stretched
and become a cougar
Just for you
It would have been so worth it

damn technology
it ruins everything
allowing me to google you later
only to find
you are WAY younger than I thought
How can this be?
all of your life experience
and old soul ways
I am old enough to be your mother!
So much for the sexual fantasy
that just seems downright disturbing now
Well
maybe you are my wake up call
to remind me
not to lose faith in mankind
there are still a few good men out there.
There is still a chance for connection.
Any chance you have a WAY older brother?

SIX DAYS OF SOLITUDE

Six days of solitude
that's what it took
to reset myself
find my balance again
meditation
yoga
paddle boarding
mountain biking
creating
no schedule
but more productive
than I've ever been
inside and out
As I age
I realize
this is my authentic life.
I need the balance of solitude
to be able to sustain
the giving I do
to my family, my friends
and through my work.
Balance restored.

ALL BY MYSELF

All by myself
just like the stubborn toddler
I want to do it
all by myself
with my own two hands
on my own two feet
with you on the sidelines
cheering me on
understanding that it's necessary
for me to do it this way
for that is when I feel
the pride of accomplishment
in having done it
all by myself

BUTTERFLIES

Butterflies remind me
I am exactly where I am supposed to be
Growing
Changing
moving forward
flying
when I am stuck
I become the caterpillar
spinning a cocoon
retreating inside
to regroup
and when I am ready
I re-emerge the butterfly

EMPATH

I am an empath
sensitive to the inner workings
of those around me.
I intuitively feel your emotions.
It's hard for me not to carry your energy.
It can be sensory overload to share space
with you for too long.
But when I am with you
I am present
emotionally walking beside you
feeling all that you are going through.
Sometimes being an empath feels too heavy.
I can no longer carry my own feelings
and the feelings of those around me.
I hibernate like a bear
retreating to the woods and water
to regain my balance.
I am an empath.

THE LIGHTHOUSE

You are a young man
heading out to sea
in search of adventure
life experience
and where you want to land next.
I watch you swim
away from the shore
embarking on this journey.
I can see a storm coming in
the waves are rougher
every now and then
I see you struggling
to not get pushed under.
You get tossed about
riding the ups and downs
of the waves.
I call out a reminder
to swim parallel to shore
if you feel caught in a rip tide.
You cannot hear me
over the roar of the ocean.

I know you don't want to turn back to shore
anyway
for this journey is so important
it is your transition to adulthood
it is meant to be turbulent
and full of lessons.
As your parent, I worry
of course I hate to see you struggle
but I remind myself
you are resilient, strong, capable
and so ready for this voyage.
It is time for me to become
the lighthouse
sending light out to you when you feel lost
or struggling to find solid ground again.
I am always here for you.
Just look toward the shore
and you will see my light
reminding you…
you always have a home
you are loved
and
I believe in you.

GOOD NIGHT WORDS

OK
That's it!
I mean it!
I am NOT turning this light on AGAIN!
I've got to get some sleep!
We can revisit this in the morning.
Crap!
I am arguing with words.
I am going to have to change the title of this book to
"Late Night Ramblings Of A Menopausal Insomniac"!

www.ingramcontent.com/pod-product-compliance
Lightning Source LLC
LaVergne TN
LVHW041547070426
835507LV00011B/978